# STEPS TO BEING BLESSED IN A RECESSION

Devotional

# STEPS TO BEING BLESSED IN A RECESSION

Devotional

Written by Levetta Booth-Rhodes, Chicago, IL.
Neu Dream Publishing, Riverside, IL

# STEPS TO BEING BLESSED IN A RECESSION

All rights reserved. No part of this book may be reproduced or transmitted in any form or by any means without written permission from the author. According to the 1976 U.S Copyright Act.

Library of Congress Control Number: 2012949659

Bibles used for scriptures New International Bible Version and King James Verison

The writing for this book began 1/2008 and completed 4/2012.

Text © 2012 Levetta Booth-Rhodes

Cover Design by Levetta Booth-Rhodes and Artavia Smith

Some Cover Photos by O'neil Peart

Author's photo by Micheal Anothony- contact via email mikephotoking@yahoo.com.

Neu Dream Publishing
P.O. Box 1402
Riverside IL 60546
www.neudreampublishing.com

ISBN: 978-0-9856114-5-3

Print in U.S.A

As I'm writing this book…

I am writing this book in faith, trusting and believing God to minister and bless all who reads this book.

## Table of Contents Page(s)

Assurance ............................................................... 1

Ask ......................................................................... 3

Belief ...................................................................... 5

Conqueror ............................................................. 8

Content .................................................................. 9

Enduring .............................................................. 10

Faith ..................................................................... 11

Fear ...................................................................... 14

Glorify .................................................................. 18

Humble ................................................................ 19

Joy ........................................................................ 21

Keeper .................................................................. 24

Knock ................................................................... 25

Live ...................................................................... 27

Love ..................................................................... 29

Redeemed ............................................................ 34

Rejoice……………………………………………………...36

Safety in the Lord…………………………………….…... 38

Sowing……………………………………………………..... 40

Spiritual Wisdom……………………………………………. 42

Trust…………………………………………………….…... 45

Victorious……………………………………………...……. 48

# Introduction

This tough economic time brings on a huge struggle in every area of one's life; at times, we don't know which way to turn. The fight for life and whether to hold on really becomes a question in one's mind. Marriages are being affected; children are being affected; people are losing their homes every day. It is getting rough. The minds of God's people have succumbed to the worldly financial difficulties, and we have lost sense of who we are and whose we are.

God came to me and said that the time has come for His people to rise and receive the comfort of knowing that He supplies every one of our needs, according to His riches and glory. We are not in a recession as long as we are obedient and tithing, even in the loss of a job. There is victory, even in the loss of a marriage. There is victory, even in the loss of a home or car. I pray that you will take this devotional and read it every day to strengthen your faith and to know that you are not alone.

This devotional is helping me as I write it, and I pray that it will help you and that your faith will grow and grow in the Lord. May you carry it with you everywhere you go, and may it be a blessing to your heart.

Be Blessed,
Levetta Rhodes

# Dedication

I first want to give all glory and honor to Jesus for all that He has done for me. When I think of His goodness, I can't do anything but praise Him. To the Almighty Father, God, who gave us His only begotten Son to die for our sins, thank You. God is my keeper in the midst of these economic times. I also want to thank my wonderful children, Elgy Booth (Shondricka) and Antoinette McClarn (Jeremy), for all the love and support that they give to me. God has blessed me with such wonderful children who have been my joy and my strength. Thank you to my lovely grandchildren, Elijah and Shamiyia, Moriah, Tamera, new additions Aiden and Jeremaiah. I love you with all my heart.

Thank you, to my special daughters, Desaray Booth, Meka, Monique. and Antoinette: my goddaughters, Ceira Levetta, Unique (RIP), Courtney Taylor, and Angel; and my godson London. I give special thanks to my Mom and Dad (Ella and J. W. Griffin), my grandparents (Cliff and Ella Ingram), and Grandma Vestella (RIP) in Oklahoma.

I would like to thank my Sisters and Brothers, for all of their support, and all of my family for being my strength. I would like to thank my pastor, John Hannah, and my first lady, Anna Hannah, and the New Life Covenant Church family

for their love, support, and encouragement to keep pushing on. Thank you to my spiritual fathers and mothers, Pastor and First Lady Meeks, Pastor and First Lady Jakes, and Pastor and First Lady Williams, as well as to Pastor Jolinda Wade and Pastor Denise Wolford (Wolf-Rod Entertainment), to Father Fleger and the St. Sabina church. Thanks to my newfound friend, Erica Savillia. I give thanks all of my friends and support people, including Ron Burge, Maurice Jackson, Sheldon Smith, and

Andre Martin. I have great respect for CEO Diane Williams of the Safer Foundation, who allowed God to use her in a way that, when she had to make cuts throughout the company, she spared staff and the services provided throughout the company and all of Safer staff. Director Andre Martin and Kira Martin, HWB, and IDOC Parole, I love you. Thank you to my great friends at ASFCME and to Ray Graham Association.

Special thanks to everyone that help put this book together. Thank you to Desaray Booth, Jermaine Peart, Moses Rivera, Marisela Esperanza, David Morrison, Micheal Anthony (of Photoking.com) and O'neil Peart for taking some of the the pictures. Thank you for allowing me to photograph you to make the cover possible. also for all the work you've done. Thank you to my editor with Compass Rose Horizon and to my Publisher Artavia Smith; the owner of Neu Dream Publishing.

I dedicate this book to all the people who are survivors of cancer (including my mom) and to people who have overcome substance abuse and turned their lives around. Thank you to all my family and to my business manager.

   -Levetta

# Assurance

As I began to write this book, I was very unsure of where God was taking me and why He wanted me to write this book. God showed me that there is going to come a time, my people, when you are going to need something that is going to assure you that He is there. A time will come about, and some people will not understand what is going on, and finances are going to be real funny. However, God said, "Your life will speak to them through My words to show them that, even in the midst of all, I still will send an assurance that I am with you and I will never leave you or forsake you." I know you will say, "How dare you tell me that? How can you assure me that I am not alone in this?"

I have been where you are right now, and although I did not want to do anything about it, He was going to be there. I felt all alone; I felt that no one was there for my children and me. I felt as if I helped everyone else and wondered when it was going to be my turn. I thought it would never change. I cried and prayed, and I thought God was taking too long to show me that He cared, but He showed up in my sleep and gave the following scripture. When I woke up, I felt a little bit stronger than I had the day before. So, I encourage you today to trust Him, and to wait on God to come.

**(NIV) Hebrews: 10:12**
For God is not unjust to forget your work and labor of love, which you have shown towards his name, in that you have ministered to the saints and do minister. And we desire that each one of you show the same diligence to the full assurance of hope until the end. That you do not become sluggish, but imitate those who, through 0faith and patience, inherit the promises.

**Prayer:**

Father God, my prayer is that You will always allow me to know that greater things are ahead, and even if things don't go the way I think they should go, give me the assurance to stand firm on Your word. In Jesus' name. Amen.

# ASK

As Christians, we sometime feel afraid or even forget that we can ask God for anything within His will, and He will grant it. Well, after He had shown me the dream about His assurance, I started to feel a little better. In a day-by-day process, things started to get a little clearer, and I was ready to take the next step. I needed some things in my home, my children needed things, and I was working from paycheck to paycheck. I wanted all the best for my children. But I always prayed for other people because I was not versed in the word of God, and I felt as if He knew what I needed. Plus, I felt like I was being selfish if I asked God for anything.

God said, "I will give you the desires of your heart," and although He may know already what we desire, Daddy just wants us to ask. That all sounded so good and easy; however, I still felt as if I should not ask for anything for myself. Then my friend, Shawn Knight of Power 92 FM, said to me, "It is not selfish when you ask God for anything; His word said, 'Ask and it shall be given, seek and ye shall find, knock and the door shall be open unto thee.'" He said, "God wants to know your heart's desires; just ask."

I remember Father J. W. used to tell me, "If you don't ask me, you won't get it," and that is what Daddy is saying to you: "Just ask me in my son's name, daughter; I will give it to you." My friend also gave me these scriptures that follow. I hope they will help you as they helped me.

**(NIV) Matthew 7:7–8**
Ask and it shall be given to you; seek and ye shall find; knock and it will be opened to you. For everyone who asks receives, and he who seeks shall find, and to him who knocks it will be opened.

**(NIV) Matthew 21:22**
And whatsoever things you ask in prayer, believe, you will receive.

**(NIV) John 11:22**
But even now I know that whatsoever you ask of God, God will give you.

**(NIV) John 16: 23–24**
And in that day will ask me nothing, most assuredly I say to you, whatever you ask the father in my name he will give you. Until now you have asked nothing in my name, ask and you will receive, that your joy may be full.

**(NIV) James 1:6**
But let him ask in faith with no doubting, for he who doubts is like a wave of the sea driven and tossed by the wind.

**(NIV) James 4:2**
You do not have because you did not ask.

**Prayer:**
Father, in the name of Jesus, I now know that I can ask You for anything. I thank You for being the Daddy that You are. I ask that You will enlarge my wisdom and knowledge in Your word. I ask You to continue to shine Your love on my children and my finances; breathe on my finances, increase them, and touch my family. I love You, Lord Jesus, and I believe You will hear my request and I trust that You will show up.

# Belief

When did I really start to believe in God for everything in my life? It was hard for me to do, especially when everything was going crazy. I had somewhat of a little belief in Him and the church; for all I had been through with the church, I had lost it for a minute. You know, at nine years old, when I was being molested by a pastor of the church, whom I thought was the person I was supposed to trust my soul with, my belief in God was gone for a minute.

Then, as I got older, it was one situation after another with the church. I had left the temple for a while, and I would like to thank my friend, Trevor Esper, who God used to bring me back to the temple. My belief in God was restored. And then the attack was on again from the members of the church.

I asked God what was going on. Why I was being accused of things I was not doing. It was crazy, so crazy. I had gone into a slight depression, and the enemy was at war again. My belief was not totally gone because I had enough belief in Him to know that He could help me out. It was at that point He moved me to a place where I could grow spiritually and mature in Him.

Now I believe in God for everything in my life, and nothing can take me away from that belief. This economy will cause you to doubt and to raise questions about where you are in Christ. Because we see where we are in Him and how to grow and become more intimate with Him. The more you study about Jesus and love Him, even in hard times and ridicule, you can believe that He will work it out. Every time Jesus did a miracle, before He did it He asked others, "Do you believe?"

So, in order to work great things in your life, just believe in Him and watch Him work.

### (NIV) Mark 11:23
For assuredly I say to you, whomever say to the mountain be removed and be cast into the sea and does not doubt in his heart, but believes that those things he says will be done, he will have whatever he says.

### (NIV) Mark 9:23
Jesus said to him, "If you can believe, all things are possible to him who believes."

### (NIV) John 6:35
Jesus said to them, "I am the bread of life, he who comes to me shall never hunger, and he who believes shall never thirst."

### (NIV) John 3:16
God so loved the world he gave his one and only son that who believes in him shall not perish but have eternal life.

### (NIV) Acts 16:31
Believe in the Lord Jesus, and you will be saved—you and your household.

### (NIV) Roman 10: 9–10
If you confess with your mouth, "Jesus is Lord," and believe in your heart that God raised him from the dead, you will be saved. For it is with the heart you believe and are justified, and it is with your mouth that you confess and are saved.

### (NIV) John 3:18
Whosoever believes in Jesus is not condemned.

**(NIV) Hebrews 11:6**
Without faith it is impossible to please God, because anyone who comes to him must believe that he exists and that he rewards those who earnestly seek him.

**Prayer:**
Father God, in the name of Jesus, it gets rough sometimes, and I feel as though all hope is gone. Please help me to believe in You for everything: for my marriage, for my job, for my children, for everything. You are my strength, and I depend only on You to make it through. I love You more than life itself. In Jesus' name I pray. Amen.

# Conqueror

It took me a long time to realize that I am my own worst enemy, not until I started seeing that everything I was touching was fading away from me. And as my marriage was drifting away, as my mindstarted to drift, as I started going into a direction that made me have to fight, it was at that time God said to me, "My child, you are more than a conqueror. Do you remember the sermon you preached about Hanna, and how she prayed and fought, and you did the illustration with the boxing glove: 'Get up, pull those gloves out of the closet, and be the winner I have made you to be.'" I started saying to myself "I am more than a conqueror, I am a winner, and I will not give up on what God has for me."

**(NIV) Romans 8:37–39**
Yet in all things we are more than conquerors through him who loved us. For I am persuaded that neither death, nor life, nor angels, nor principalities, nor power, nor things present, nor any other created thing shall be able to separate us from the love of God which is in Christ Jesus our Lord.

**Prayer:**
Father God, thank You for Your love and Your kindness, for showing me that I am a winner. I am a conqueror. I can run until the end. Thank You, Jesus, for loving me; even when I am weak, You gave me strength. I love in Jesus' name Amen.

# Content

Hey, you, being content in a situation is very hard. We become anxious, we become antsy, and we lose focus on the bigger picture. Paul said in Philippians 4:10–11 (NIV): "But I rejoice in the Lord greatly, that now at last your care for me has flourished again, though you surely did care, but you lacked opportunity. Not that I speak in regards to my needs for I have learned that whatsoever state I am in, to be content."

**(NIV) 1Timothy 6:6–8**
Now Godliness with contentment is great, for we brought nothing into this world, and it is certain we can carry nothing out. And having food and clothing with these we shall be content**.**

**Prayer:**
Father, help me in the name of Jesus to not complain. Help me to be an encourager, even in the midst of these economic times. Help me to be content and to pull someone else up to be the fighter that I am, for I pray for that very situation that is worse than mine is.

# Enduring

So now, we are conquerors, and we know that we can be content in whatever state we are in. There is no possible reason we cannot endure. We can run on to see what the end is going to be. However, we all slip a little bit, so here are some enduring scriptures to get you through.

**(NIV) Psalm 30:5**
For the anger is but for a moment, but His favor is for life; weeping may endure for a night, but joy comes in the morning.

**Prayer:**
Lord God, please give me enduring power to fight and to wait patiently for my change to come. In Jesus' name. Amen.

# Faith

It is very hard to accomplish any goal or anything in life, especially in an economy like this. We are told to have faith. Please, how can we in this world? With no jobs, no finances. Have faith, you say. My husband is gone, my wife left me, or better yet, he or she has not left but is going out every night with another person. Faith is the last thing on my mind right now, how dare you tell me about faith. I know this is what you might say. I know it is hard because, as I write this book, I have a job. The economy is bad, and I am still getting overtime, so who am I to tell you about faith? The right person. I have faith to believe that God can carry me through anything.

I have been separated for two years, and while my husband is out there doing what he said God told him to do, I still stand on the word of God to work that out for His glory. Is it easy? No, because you deal with the thought of waiting and then not knowing which way to go, seeing your life at a standstill until you decide to do something different. I stand on my faith with my job because when I asked, "God, should I get a second job?" He told me "no" and started blessing me with overtime. And I have been getting it ever since. So, my faith is carrying me through it all.

The Bible calls the people of God to have faith. Believe now more than you have ever believed; even in these times, you can be sure doubt is not an option. God is worth keeping.

Here are some scriptures to help you through and to step out with faith even more.

of Jerusalem! Have faith in the LORD your God and you will be upheld; have faith in his prophets and you will be successful."

## (NIV) Habakkuk 2:4
See, he is puffed up; his desires are not upright—but the righteous will live by his faith.

## (NIV) Matthew 6:30
If that is how God clothes the grass of the field, which is here today and tomorrow is thrown into the fire, will he not much more clothe you, O you of little faith?

## (NIV) Matthew 8:10
When Jesus heard this, he was astonished and said to those following him, "I tell you the truth, I have not found anyone in Israel with such great faith."

## (NIV) Matthew 8:26
He replied, "You of little faith, why are you so afraid?" Then he got up and rebuked the winds winds and the waves, and it was completely calm.

## (NIV) Matthew 9:2
Some men brought to him a paralytic, lying on a mat. When Jesus saw their faith, he said to the paralytic, "Take heart, son; your sins are forgiven."

## (NIV) Matthew 14:31
Immediately Jesus reached out his hand and caught him. "You of little faith," he said, "why did you doubt?"

## (NIV) Mark 4:40
He said to his disciples, "Why are you so afraid? Do you still have no faith?"

**(NIV) 2 Chronicle 20:20**
Early in the morning they left for the Desert of Tekoa. As they set out, Jehoshaphat stood and said, "Listen to me, Judah and people

**(NIV) Mark 11:22**
"Have faith in God," Jesus answered.

**(NIV) Luke 17:6**
He replied, "If you have faith as small as a mustard seed, you can say to this mulberry tree, 'Be uprooted and planted in the sea,' and it will obey you."

**(NIV) Acts 14: 22**
Strengthening the disciples and encouraging them to remain true to the faith. "We must go through many hardships to enter the kingdom of God," they said.

**(NIV) Hebrews 11:1**
Now Faith is the substance of things hoped for and the evidence of things not seen.

**(KJV) Psalm 33:22**
Let thy mercy, O Lord, be upon us, according as we hope in thee.

**Prayer:**
Father God, all the days may seem dim. God Strengthen my faith to continue to stand and believe, and to have the faith the size of a mustard seed to know that it.

# Fear

Now, as I got into the business of my husband leaving me, I referred to a hurt that I never thought I had to feel. I was scared to even think about being alone and facing another relationship. I was hurt, yes, and scared, even though in the back of my mind I knew this was of God. Now I don't glorify leaving your spouse because if you have a great man in your life or a great woman, hold on to your marriage. For six years, I prayed for God to give me favor in my husband's eyes, and it never happened.

I also began to pray for the woman he left me for. I prayed for her marriage to work so she could get out of mine, and that my husband would return home. I was afraid to move on with my life, and I had fooled myself into thinking I needed him financially. When we were together, I never got anything from him. Fear of being alone got me to a point that I was accepting anything from him, and he was being cold to me.

I never realized that God was not answering my plea for Him to give me favor because, all that time, my husband was the one being obedient to what God had told him and I was not. For so many times, I had been hurt by men, since I was five years of age. I was scared to move on.

I asked God to remove the fear, and He did. I able to see clearly and to see that what was happening was God, and I needed to step back and look at things and move forward to the next level of my life. Here are some scriptures that can help you as they helped me.

## (NIV) Deuteronomy 7:19
You saw with your own eyes the great trials, the miraculous signs and wonders, the mighty hand and outstretched arm,

which the LORD your God brought you out. The LORD your God will do the same to all the peoples you now fear.

**(NIV) Job 3:25**
What I feared has come upon me; what I dreaded has happened to me

**(NIV) Job 5:21**
You will be protected from the lash of the tongue, and need not fear when destruction comes.

**(NIV) Job 11:15**
Then you will lift up your face without shame; you will stand firm and without fear.

**(NIV) Job 39:22**
He laughs at fear, afraid of nothing; he does not shy away from the sword.

**(NIV) Psalm 23:4**
Even though I walk through the valley of the shadow of death, I will fear no evil, for you are with me; your rod and your staff, they comfort me.

**(NIV) Psalm 27:1**
The LORD is my light and my salvation—whom shall I fear? The LORD is the stronghold of my life—of whom shall I be afraid?

**(NIV) Psalm 27:3**
Though an army besiege me, my heart will not fear; though war break out against me, even then will I be confident.

**((NIV) Psalm 34:4**
I sought the LORD, and he answered me; he delivered me from all my fears.

**NIV) Psalms 34:7**
The angel of the LORD encamps around those who fear him, and he delivers them.

**(NIV) Psalm 34:9**
Fear the LORD, you his saints, for those who fear him lack nothing.

**(NIV) Psalm 49:5**
Why should I fear when evil days come, when wicked deceivers surround me—?

**(NIV) Psalm 112:7**
He will have no fear of bad news; his heart is steadfast, trusting in the LORD.

**(NIV) Psalm 112:8**
His heart is secure, he will have no fear; in the end he will look in triumph on his foes.

**(NIV) Psalm 67:7**
God will bless us, and all the ends of the earth will fear him.

**(NIV) Psalm 91:5**
You will not fear the terror of night, nor the arrow that flies by day,

**(NIV) Psalm 111:10**
The fear of the LORD is the beginning of wisdom; all who follow

his precepts have good understanding. To him belongs eternal praise.

**(NIV) I Corinthians 16:10**
If Timothy comes, see to it that he has nothing to fear while he is with you, for he is carrying on the work of the Lord, just as I am.

**(NIV) I Corinthians 16:10**
If Timothy comes, see to it that he has nothing to fear while he is with you, for he is carrying on the work of the Lord, just as I am.

**Prayer:**
Father God, I thank You for Your greatness, and I know that You have not given me the spirit of fear. I pray that I continue to realize that if I continue to fear You, I am promised great things. I love You and I know You are there. In Jesus' name. Amen.

# Glorify

How awesome to know that even in the midst of all the things going on, we can glorify God's presence and His love, protection, and kindness towards us. I love Him so much.

**(NIV) Psalm 34:3**
Glorify the LORD with me; let us exalt his name together.

**(NIV) Psalms 63:3**
Because your love is better than life, my lips will glorify you.

**(NIV) Psalms 86:12**
I will praise you, O Lord my God, with all my heart; I will glorify your name forever.

**Prayer:**
Holy one, awesome one, all mighty God you are great. Thou are holy, thou art wonderful, you are my friend, you are my peace, you are the love of my soul, you are my king , my Lord, my joy, my waymaker, my provider, my healer, my mind regulator, my heart fixer, my disciplinarian, my corrector, my strength, the one who guides me, the one loves in my mess, the one who never gives up on me, the who never leaves me, the one who educates me, the one who elevates me, my friend, the one who send me, (tongues). I glorify your names in the mist of my financial difficulty, in the mist of my pain, in the mist of my divorce, in the mist my children acting up, in the mist of it all I stand, I stand in Jesus name I pray Amen.

# Humble

In all tests and in all things, please remain Humble in everything, even in the midst of this recession. Yeah, I know you say "it is crazy" and "how in the world can she say that?" You think I must not have lost my job, I must not have lost a husband, and my finances must be off the chain. You are so right. In this recession, I have not lost my job. And in this recession, I can say my finances are okay. I have lost my husband, but I have accepted that my loss and my pain will not dictate how and if I should remain humble during these times and any other time. Because if I remain humble, I can hear what God has for me. So, in all, please remain humble until God shows up. God has expressed His ways of showing us how and why we should be humble.

Please see the following scriptures.

**(NIV) Deuteronomy 8:3**
He humbled you, causing you to hunger and then feeding you with manna, which neither you nor your fathers had known, to teach you that man does not live on bread alone but on every word that comes from the mouth of the LORD.

**(NIV) Deuteronomy 8:16**
He gave you manna to eat in the desert, something your fathers had never known, to humble and to test you so that in the end it might go well with you.

**(NIV) 2 Kings 22:19**
Because your heart was responsive and you humbled yourself before the LORD when you heard what I have spoken against this place and its people, that they would become accursed and be laid waste, and because you tore your robes and wept in my presence, I heard you, declares the LORD.

**NIV) 2 Chronicles 7:14**
If my people, who are called by my name, will humble themselves and pray and seek my face and turn from their wicked ways, then will I hear from heaven and will forgive their sin and will heal their land.

**(NIV) 2 Chronicles 33:12**
In his distress he sought the favor of the LORD his God and humbled himself greatly before the God of his fathers.

**(NIV) Job 8:7**
Your beginnings will seem humble, so prosperous will your future be.

**Prayer:**
Lord God, in the name of Jesus, please help me to remain humble even in the midst of my situation, knowing that You are God mighty and You have the key to fix and answer all things. I trust You and I wait patiently to hear Your voice. In Jesus' name.

# Joy

Hey, the Joy of the Lord is my strength. Yes, He has humbled me and my spirit, and I felt His joy moving inside of me. I get joy when I think about what the Lord has done for me. Well, I guess you see where I am going with this. Yes, joy. It is my prayer that you will be in full joy, even in the midst of these times.

**(NIV) 1 Chronicles 29:17**
I know, my God, that you test the heart and are pleased with integrity. All these things have I given willingly and with honest intent. And now I have seen with joy how willingly your people who are here have given to you.

**(NIV) Job 8:21**
He will yet fill your mouth with laughter and your lips with shouts of joy.

**(NIV) Job 33:26**
He prays to God and finds favor with him, he sees God's face and shouts for joy; he is restored by God to his righteous state.

**(NIV) Job 38:7**
While the morning stars sang together and all the angels shouted for joy?

**(NIV) Psalm 4:7**
You have filled my heart with greater joy than when their grain and new wine abound.

**(NIV) Psalm 5:11**
But let all who take refuge in you be glad; let them ever sing for joy. Spread your protection over them that those who love your name may rejoice in you.

**(NIV) Psalm 20:5**
We will shout for joy when you are victorious and will lift up our banners in the name of our God. May the LORD grant all your requests.

**(NIV) Psalm 21**
O LORD, the king rejoices in your strength. How great is his joy in the victories you give!

**(NIV) Psalm 21:6**
Surely, you have granted him eternal blessings and made him glad with the joy of your presence.

**(NIV) Psalm 28:7**
The LORD is my strength and my shield; my heart trusts in him, and I am helped. My heart leaps for joy and I will give thanks to him in song.

**(NIV) Psalm 30:11**
You turned my wailing into dancing; you removed my sackcloth and clothed me with joy.

**(NIV) Psalm 35:27**
May those who delight in my vindication shout for joy and gladness; may they always say, "The LORD be exalted, who delights in the well-being of his servant."

**(NIV) Psalm 43:4**
Then will I go to the altar of God, O God, my joy and my delight. I will praise you with the harp, O God, my God.

**(NIV) Psalm 90:14**
Satisfy us in the morning with your unfailing love, that we may sing for joy and be glad all our days.

**(NIV) Psalm 94:19**
When anxiety was great within me, your consolation brought joy to my soul.

**(NIV) Psalm 100:1**
For giving thanks. Shout for joy to the LORD, all the earth.

**(NIV) Psalm 100:2**
Worship the LORD with gladness; come before him with joyful songs.

**(NIV) Psalm 106:5**
That I may enjoy the prosperity of your chosen ones, that I may share in the joy of your nation and join your inheritance in giving praise.

**(NIV) Psalm 118:15**
Shouts of joy and victory resound in the tents of the righteous: "The LORD's right hand has done mighty things!"

**(NIV) Psalm 126:2**
Our mouths were filled with laughter, our tongues with songs of joy. Then it was said among the nations, "The LORD has done great things for them."

I can go on and on about the joy you find in the scriptures, but I must leave you to continue to shout. When I think of His goodness and all He has done for me, my soul cries out, "Hallelujah!"
This is my prayer. In Jesus's name. Amen.

# Keeper

I am a firm believer that God is a keeper, and that He would hold you in the midst of everything. When all the drama is going on around you, He will keep you in an isolated peace where it won't even touch you. Jesus will keep you even though they are letting off around you. God will touch that CEO's heart, and he or she will find other ways to cut, other than cutting staff. Trust God and know that He is a keeper. Come on, let me show you.

**(KJV) Psalm 121:5**
The LORD is thy keeper: the LORD is thy shade upon thy right hand.

**(KJV) Isaiah 26:3**
Thou wilt keep him in perfect peace, whose mind is stayed on thee: because he trusteth in thee.

**Prayer:**
Father God, I love You so much. I know that You love me. You are my keeper in the midst of everything going on. I trust You, Lord, to keep me. God, even if I lose my job, You are my provider. You are my way maker. I love You; I love You so much. A keeper. A keeper.A keeper. I praise Your name. In Jesus' name, I pray. Amen

# Knock

I know you are thinking, "W here does this fit in?" I know you are because I did when God revealed it to me. He said, "Levetta, knock." I took my hand and started to move it in a knocking position, and then kept knocking. As I knocked, it came to me: The door is opening. And as I continued to knock, my destiny appeared to me even more. God said to me, "If you keep knocking, the door to greater places, greater things, will open." Tears ran down my face, and I was ready. So, as you read these scriptures, start knocking and see what door God is trying to take you through.

### (KJV) Matthew 7:7
Ask and it shall be given you; seek, and ye shall find; knock, and it shall be opened unto you.

### (KJV) Matthew 7:8
For every one that asketh receiveth; and he that seeketh findeth; and to him that knocketh it shall be opened.

### (KJV) Luke 11:9
And I say unto you, ask, and it shall be given you; seek, and ye shall find; knock, and it shall be opened unto you.

### (KJV) Luke 12:36
And ye yourselves like unto men that wait for their lord, when he will return from the wedding; that when he cometh and knocketh, they may open unto him immediately.

### (KJV) Revelation 3:20
Behold, I stand at the door, and knock: if any men hear my voice, and open the door, I will come in to him, and will sup with him, and he with me.

## Prayer:

Father, Sweet Jesus, I first want to say, "Thank You." I first want to say, "I love You." Father, You know in Your word, when You said ask and it shall be given, seek and ye shall be found, knock and the door shall be open unto me—for every closed door, God, You open two. I am a winner, and I knock that I will not be knocked down without a fight. I love You and I praise You. In Jesus' name, I pray. Amen.

# Live

You gave up. You have thrown in the towel on your marriage, your child, your job search. Whatever the situation may be, you have sulked yourself into a hole and hidden your face and said, "God has forgotten." The time has come for you to get up and stop the pity party; rise above the adversities in your life, grasp hold of life! Rise up, my son, rise up, my daughter, and live, live, live!

**(KJV) Numbers 14:21**
But as truly as I live, all the earth shall be filled with the glory of the LORD.

**(KJV) Deuteronomy 5:24**
And ye said, Behold, the LORD our God hath shewed us his glory and his greatness, and we have heard his voice out of the midst of the fire: we have seen this day that God doth talk with man, and he liveth.

**(KJV) Deuteronomy 5:33**
Ye shall walk in all the ways which the LORD your God hath commanded you, that ye may live, and that it may be well with you, and that ye may prolong your days in the land which ye shall possess.

**(KJV) Deuteronomy 30:16**
In that I command thee this day to love the LORD thy God, to walk in his ways, and to keep his commandments and his statutes and his judgments, that thou mayest live and multiply: and the LORD thy God shall bless thee in the land whither thou goest to possess it.

**Prayer:**
Father, help me as I cry and go through the trials, pain, and hurt of losing my ( fill in ). I can't fight any more. I ask You, God, to help me to live again, to help me regain my strength, integrity, and faith. I love You so much, and I thank You for my life. I believe Your word. You said You would give me life, and it is more abundant. In Jesus' name, I pray. Amen.

# Love

"Hey, you" are the famous words my supervisor Ron Burge always says. He says them in a way that lets you know that today is going to be a great day. He says them with love, as a love for his daughter; and even in the midst of what surrounds him, he still shows that kind of love. We should be as he is in that even in the midst of it all, we will continue to show love and feel the love of Jesus around us.

We should not be troubled. Our hearts should be filled with the love that Jesus gives every day. I can truly say that at some point in life, it is hard to love the one that has hurt us. Not everyone can be a Mr. Burge. At times, we have been hurt so bad by people that we come to lose sight of what love is. We are mad at the person who has let us go on a job, when really we should look at why and what God may be doing in that situation for you.

Jesus loved in spite of us; and He loved so much that He gave His life for us. How many are willing to do that? Give of yourself to someone who you say hurt you. We cannot move on unless we live in love. I pray for my husband, and he has been gone many years no calls, and I don't know where he is right now; however, that will not stop me from loving him as a person. It is so hard, but we cannot be Christ-like if we don't walk in love.

**(KJV) Deuteronomy 7:9**
Know therefore that the LORD thy God, he is God, the faithful God, which keepeth covenant and mercy with them that love him and keep his commandments to a thousand generations.

**(KJV) Deuteronomy 7:13**
And he will love thee, and bless thee, and multiply thee: he will also bless the fruit of thy womb, and the fruit of thy land, thy corn.

and thy wine, and thine oil, the increase of thy kine, and the flocks of the sheep, in the land which he sware unto thy fathers to give thee.

**(KJV) Deuteronomy 23:5**
Nevertheless the LORD thy God would not hearken unto Balaam; but the LORD thy God turned the curse into a blessing unto thee, because the LORD thy God loved thee.

**(KJV) Deuteronomy 30:6**
And the LORD thy God will circumcise thine heart, and the heart of thy seed, to love the LORD thy God with all thine heart, and with all thy soul, that thou mayest live.

**(KJV) Joshua 22:5**
But take diligent heed to do the commandment and the law, which Moses the servant of the LORD charged you, to love the LORD your God, and to walk in all his ways, and to keep his commandments, and to cleave unto him, and to serve him with all your heart and with all your soul.

**(KJV) Judges 16:15**
And she said unto him, How canst thou say, I love thee, when thine heart is not with me? Thou hast mocked me these three times, and hast not told me wherein thy great strength lieth.

**(KJV) Psalm 5:11**
But let all those that put their trust in thee rejoice: let them ever shout for joy, because thou defendest them: let them also that love thy name be joyful in thee.

**(KJV) Psalm 18:1**
I will love thee, O LORD, my strength.

**(KJV) Psalm 31:23**
O love the LORD, all ye his saints: for the LORD preserveth the faithful, and plentifully rewardeth the proud doer.

**(KJV) Psalm 33:5**
He loveth righteousness and judgment: the earth is full of the goodness of the LORD.

**(KJV) Psalm 70:4**
Let all those that seek thee rejoice and be glad in thee: and let such as love thy salvation say continually, Let God be magnified.

**(KJV) Psalm 97:10**
Ye that love the LORD hate evil: he preserveth the souls of his saints; he delivereth them out of the hand of the wicked.

**(KJV) Psalm 109:4**
For my love they are my adversaries: but I give myself unto prayer.

**(KJV) Psalm 116:1**
I love the LORD, because he hath heard my voice and my supplications.

**(KJV) Psalm 119:165**
Great peace have they which love thy law: and nothing shall offend them.

**(KJV) Psalm 145:20**
The LORD preserveth all them that love him: but all the wicked will he destroy.

**(KJV) Song of Solomon 1:4**
Draw me, we will run after thee: the king hath brought me into his chambers: we will be glad and rejoice in thee, we will

remember thy love more than wine: the upright love thee.

**(KJV) John 15:9**
As the Father hath loved me, so have I loved you: continue ye in my love.

**(KJV) John 15:13**
Greater love hath no man than this, that a man lay down his life for his friends.

**(KJV) John 16:27**
For the Father himself loveth you, because ye have loved me, and have believed that I came out from God.

**(KJV) Romans 8:28**
And we know that all things work together for good to them that love God, to them who are the called according to his purpose.

**(KJV) Romans 12:9**
Let love be without dissimulation. Abhor that which is evil; cleave to that which is good.

**(KJV) 1 Corinthians 2:9**
But as it is written, eye hath not seen, nor ear heard neither have entered into the heart of man, the things which God hath prepared for them that love him.

**(KJV) 1 Corinthians 16:24**
My love is with you all in Christ Jesus. Amen.

**(KJV) 2 Corinthians 2:4**
For out of much affliction and anguish of heart I wrote unto you with many tears; not that ye should be grieved, but that ye might know the love which I have more abundantly unto you.

### (KJV) Corinthians 6:6
By pureness, by knowledge, by long-suffering, by kindness, by theHoly Ghost, by love unfeigned.

### (KJV) 2 Corinthians 8:24
Wherefore shew ye to them, and before the churches, the proof of your love, and of our boasting on your behalf.

### (KJV) 2 Corinthians 13:11
Finally, brethren, farewell. Be perfect, be of good comfort, be of one mind, live in peace; and the God of love and peace shall be with you.

### (KJV) Galatians 5:22
But the fruit of the Spirit is love, joy, peace, longsuffering, gentleness, goodness, faith.

### (KJV) Ephesians 5:2
And walk in love, as Christ also hath loved us, and hath given himself for us an offering and a sacrifice to God for a sweet-smelling savour.

### (KJV) Ephesians 6:23
Peace be to the brethren, and love with faith, from God the Father and the Lord Jesus Christ.

**Prayer:**
Oh Great God, my God, blood of Jesus. You loved me and cared for me and kept me. You gave up so much for me and all I did was turn my back on You. I pray that my love will grow and, in spite of how people treat me, I will still walk in love with them. I ask You to keep me rooted and grounded in love. For Your word says, "It is by love and kindness have I drawn thee." I ask that You continue to keep me and hold me. In Jesus' name. Amen

# Redeemed

**Psalms 107:2** says, "Let the redeemed of the Lord say so," I attended the Bill Winston Living Word School of Ministry and have never been so excited about learning before in my life. You talk about some purging and cleansing and rebirthing in the newness of the word! Don't get me wrong. My pastor, Daniel X. Smith, gives an awesome word, and he also attended the School of Ministry, so he is not afraid of sending us out to learn somewhere else. Well, while in there, I felt so redeemed and rejuvenated, that now I can say that scripture with authority: "Let the redeemed of the Lord say so."

I walk with a new grace every day. I run the race like no one can stop me, learning everything from church history to vision writing to experiencing a greater faith like never before. As Pastor Donnie McClurkin says, "I'm Walking in authority." Yes, I am redeemed, bought with a price. Jesus has changed my whole life. I am stronger and mightier than I think. I am redeemed. I am redeemed. Glory to God.

Here are some scriptures to keep you focused on who you

**(KJV) Psalms 107:2**
Let the redeemed of the LORD say so, whom He has redeemed from the hand of the adversary.

**(KJV) Psalm 106:10**
He saved them from the hand of the foe; from the hand of the enemy he redeemed them.

**(NIV) Isaiah 62:12**
They will be called the Holy People, the Redeemed of the LORD; and you will be called Sought After, the City No Longer Deserted.

**Prayer:**
Father God, thank You for being my redeemer. It is because of You am redeemed. I can live again. I can breathe again. I am alive again. And I thank You for Pastor Bill Winston and Pastor Derrick Bright and for all of the School of Ministry staff. Bless them in abundance. In Jesus' name. Amen.

# Rejoice

The greatest thing in life is to know that you can rejoice in the Lord.Not knowing where my next payment was going to come from while being in the School of Ministry, the greatest thing was rejoicing and not knowing how my mission trip was going to get paid for. So all I had was my praise. People tend to tell me I act as if I have never been through anything and that I live in a dream. What they fail to realize is that they don't know how I rejoice because God brought me out of a sexual abuse act at the age of five while in a preschool on the West Side of Chicago. They don't know I rejoice because Jesus' blood kept my mind after a sexual abuse from a pastor of a church at the age of nine. They don't know I rejoiced after having a child taken from me at an abortion clinic, after I was advised by church members to do so. I rejoice because God's mercy kept me in the midst of an adulterous relationship when I could have been dead. There is more. There is more; however, I decided to allow myself to let my praise cover it up and let God do what He needs to do in my life.

So I've rejoiced in the Lord always. Yes, I've had some crying nights. Yes, I've had some upsetting days. But God kept me, so I rejoiced and praised God. It was not until I attended the School of Ministry that God started to reveal to me that the enemy was trying to take me out at the age of nine. If I would have stopped praising God and stopped going to church after the sexual abuse, I would not be here now to tell my story and help someone else. So I say to you, rejoice in the Lord, even when it doesn't look like you are going to make it.

Here are some scriptures to assist you in bringing your praise out more.

**(MSG) Deuteronomy 26:11**
Then place it in the presence of God, your God. Prostrate yourselves in the presence of God, Your God. And rejoice! Celebrate all good things that God, your God has given you and your family; you and the Levite and the foreigner who lives with you.

**(KJV) Psalm 33:1**
Rejoice in the Lord, o ye righteous, for praise is comely for the upright.

**(KJV) Psalm 33:2**
Praise the Lord with the harp; sing unto him with the psaltery and an instrument of ten strings.

**(KJV) Psalm 23**
The LORD is my shepherd; I shall not want. He maketh me to lie down in green pastures: he leadeth me beside the still waters. He restoreth my soul: he leadeth me in the paths of righteousness for his name's sake. Yea, though I walk through the valley of the shadow of death, I will fear no evil: for thou art with me; thy rod and thy staff they comfort me. Thou preparest a table before me in the presence of mine enemies: thou anointest my head with oil; my cup runneth over. Surely goodness and mercy shall follow me all the days of my life: and I will dwell in the house of the LORD for ever.

# Safety in the Lord

I must say that, in these days, I have found more and more to remind myself that there is safety in Jesus. As times gets harder, the people of God are covered safely in the Lord.

Now, I would be lying if I tell you that I don't see the times we are in. And I would say to you that at one point in my life I was scared; however, I can pick up this book and go back to read some of the things I have written and used for myself. God has not given me the spirit of fear. I had to realize that no matter what is going on around me, I am safely tucked in the arms of the Lord. I know that no weapon that the enemy tries to form will prosper. God gave me power to tread upon the serpent and nothing will harm me. I am protected; you are protected by the Blood of Jesus at all times. So know that no matter what comes and who tries to come against you, you are safe in the Lord's arms.

**(MSG) Proverbs 18:10**
God's name is a place of protection—good people can run there and be safe.

**(MSG) 1 Chronicles 4:9**
Jabez was a better man than his brothers, a man of honor. His mother had named him Jabez (Oh, the pain!), saying, "A painful birth! I bore him in great pain!" Jabez prayed to the God of Israel: "Bless me, O bless me! Give me land, large tracts of land. And provide your personal protection—don't let evil hurt me." God gave him what he asked.

**(MSG) Psalm 34:7**
God's angel sets up a circle of protection around us while we pray.

**(MSG) Isaiah 27:2**
"At that same time, a fine vineyard will appear. There's something to sing about! I, God, tend it. I keep it well-watered. I keep careful watch over it so that no one can damage it. I'm not angry. I care. Even if it gives me thistles and thorn bushes, I'll just pull them out and burn them up.

Let that vine cling to me for safety, let it find a good and whole life with me, let it hold on for a good and whole life."

**(MSG) Jeremiah 33:14**
"Watch for this: The time is coming'—God's Decree—'when I will keep the promise I made to the families of Israel and Judah. When that time comes, I will make a fresh and true shoot sprout from the David-Tree. He will run this country honestly and fairly. He will set things right. That's when Judah will be secure and Jerusalem live in safety. The motto for the city will be, "God Has Set Things Right for Us." God has made it clear that there will al ways be a descendant of David ruling the people of Israel and that there will always be Levitical priests on hand to offer burnt offerings, present grain offerings, and carry on the sacrificial worship in my honor.'"

**Prayer:**
Father God, my protector and sustainer, my armor, my strength. Lord, You told me You will fight my battles; day to day, I learn to trust You even more. I know that You are a keeper and You love me. So I don't worry about the recession because I am Your child. I don't worry about where my next meal is going to come from because You are my provider. I don't worry about times getting worse or getting robbed; You protect me from seen and unseen danger. You carry me in Your arms, and the two angels You have on each side of me guard and protect me from all harm. Thank You for protecting me from myself. I love You and I praise You. In Jesus' name. Amen.

# Sowing

I would not be surprised if you are saying to yourself right now, as you see this topic of sowing, "Ha! Sowing, I can barely sow in to me. I can barely see the light of day sowing, she got her nerves." Wait, wait, wait. Slow down. Let me help you out with sowing. When we hear "sowing," we always think about money, and that is not always the case. Money is good; however, I was not always there to be able to give, so I sowed in my time.

I always gave back in sowing time to the church, volunteering as a servant on ministries. And also, I sow into Endure Productions (Kim Tyler) under the leadership of my boss and director, Andre Martin, as security for their events. I also sow as security and backstage for St. Sabina and Inspiration 1390 Peace Jam. I also sow into Wolf Rod Entertainment in Texas, for the coordinating of the domestic violence march every year in Chicago during the first week in June. I am trying to get you to see here how it's important to give of your time to sowing into someone else's ministry; and as God blesses you financially, then you sow into that way.

Sowing financially is awesome to me; I just love to give to the point that it hurts me when I can't give. However, this is just me; sowing into other people's ministries makes life that much easier for me. In **IICorinthians 9:6**, the Bible says, "But this I say, he which soweth sparingly shall also reap sparingly, and he which sow bountifully shall reap also bountifully." Now we hear that scripture, but amazingly, as I read on, this one seems to be more befitting for sowing your time. **II Corinthians 9:10–12**: "Now he that ministereth unto the sower both minister bread for your food, and multiply your seed sown, and increase the fruit of your righteousness; being enriched in everything to all bountifulness, which causeth through us thanks giving to God." That tells me that you can minister unto someone in every way and they can sow that seed into someone else's life, you are called blessed and that is awesome. Trust me, I know and believe that to be very true—that goes with ministering unto the man or woman of God, the sick, the poor, and when you minister unto the people of God, you are blessed.

Sowing seed is great, and when you give it not grudgingly or of necessity, you are blessed; that mean when you give without a motive behind it or an attitude of "what can I get out of it," you are blessed. When you sow into someone and can do it without a thank you, sometimes God will do just what He said He would do in your life. That also goes for tithing and offering. There are so many ministries across the world to sow into, some in your community; try it and see.

**Prayer:**
Father God, I love You so much. Jesus, I am so grateful to know that You are my life and my world. Father, I want to be a giver and a sower into people's lives. Breathe on my finances, help me to be more committed to sowing time and volunteering wherever needed. I pray You enlarge my territory and my finances. Bless me in every way of my life. I decree in Jesus' name I will be a sower; I am a giver. In Jesus' name. Amen.

# Spiritual Wisdom

I will tell you a little secret. Now, don't you tell anybody. I am going to let you in my world for a minute. Let me tell you: I am now a divorced woman, and when I got married, I did not use any wisdom at all. Even though the signs were there, I continued to do what I thought would help my ex-husband. My ex-husband was a heroin user. Did I know this before we got married? Yes! Did I think that I could save him? Yes! Did I consult God in this? No! I made the situation worse because I did not know what to do or how to handle someone using drugs.

Now, here is the scary part. Two weeks prior to seeing my husband, I had a dream. Now, I took the dream as we were meant to be together, and God would save him and clean him through me. Yes, he got saved, and I think he is not using anymore. But here is a twist.

That dream was warning me about two things. I was supposed to help him, not marry him, and he was also to be the person that God used for my punishment for something. When did I get all this wisdom about this? It was many years later, after being separated and going to the Bill Winston Living Christian Center School of Ministry. I know you thought I was going to hit on finances; however, I used this situation to tell you in this time and age that we need to be very careful about the choices we make.

The pressures of the economy can make us do crazy things and get into situations that are not ordained by God. Self can make us do things that are not of God. When the bills are dueand the food is low, we panic; and when we pray to God, what we think is the answer is not.

God won't send us someone that we would have sex with to get taken care of. There was this man that is still chasing me today, and what is so funny about the situation is that he said, "If you give me some, maybe I could do this and that for you." " That man has been chasing me for many years; now, even in that situation, he will try to make you feel as though you are holding out all in vain by saying, "Hum, Sally Mae put out and he bought her a car." Sally Mae put out, and he did this and that. Well, that's Sally Mae, and if it worked for Sally Mae, that is okay; however, I used spiritual wisdom to fight that battle. The earth is the Lord's and the fullness thereof. Now, I am not knocking Sally Mae. But Levetta Booth can't do it. Women, we tend to go find sugar daddies to take care of our needs; men, you don't want another man or woman to take care of you.

I had to use spiritual wisdom, which gave me some practical knowledge to take care of my children and me. I had to go and repent for stepping out of His will into that marriage. I had to start budgeting and become a good steward over everything that God has given me. Over my finances, over my children, over my grandbabies, over my job, over my car, over my relationship, over GMI Ministries, over the family empowerment conference over every area of my life. I got tired of being hurt and lacking, and I was not going to be a product of this economy; and the real man in my life, God, keeps me better than anybody could.

Now I am going to pray with you that God will grant you wisdom in every area of your life, and that you may prosper in it greatly. And because of this wisdom, God will bless you with much

Here is some scripture to help you may you be filled with great knowledge,

**(KJV) Psalm 111:10.**
The fear of the Lord is the beginning of wisdom; all they that do

keep his commandments: his praise endureth forever.

**(KJV) James 1:5**
If any man lack wisdom, let him ask of God, that giveth men liberally, and upbraideth not; and it shall be given.

**(KJV) Proverbs 5: 5–7.**
Get Wisdom, get understanding: forget it not; neither decline from the words of my mouth. Forsake her not, and she shall preserve thee: love her, and she shall keep thee. Wisdom is the principle thing; therefore get wisdom: and with all thy getting get understanding.

**(KJV) Proverbs 9:9–11.**
Give instruction to a wise man, and he will be yet wiser; teach a j ust man, and he will increase in learning. The fear of the Lord, is the beginning of wisdom; and the knowledge of the holy is understanding.For by me thy days shall be multiplied, and the years of thy life shall be increased.

**Prayer:**
Heavenly father, we love You so much that even in wrong decisions and mistakes in our lives that we make, You still loved on us. Thank You, Father; You said in Your word that the fear of the Lord is the beginning of wisdom. All who follow Your precept have good understanding, to You belongs eternal praise. You also said, God, that wisdom is supreme, therefore, get wisdom. Father, we come for understanding and knowledge of Your word and Your will for our lives. We ask that You help us understand Your purpose and trust that you're in this economy for your people. I pray that wisdom will show us how to start our own businesses, how to invest, how to receive the supernatural gifts from You. Lord, we praise You and thank You in Jesus' name. Amen.

# Trust

Getting a divorce in this economy is not easy. If ever there was a time I needed to trust God more, it is now—not for finances, but for guidance, trust, loving again, and a relationship. Everything in my life. Did I want to start dating again? Let me keep it real; part of me did want to date again, and a great part of me wanted to wait because I was scared of what I would run in to. So for many years I held on to a marriage until I was ready to really just focus on God and His word.

I still needed to get things out of me. Then God had to start preparing me for the things He has for He and I to do. So, I trust God for my relationships and for making sure I don't enter into a bad situation because of finances and this economy. The economy takes a toll on every area of anyone's life. If you allow it, it will cause divorce or push you into a relationship just because you need the money; it will cause you to do crazy things out of your character and cause you to think that it is right.

I trusted God to bring me through nine months of the School of Ministry. At the time I started the School of Ministry, I had just started a new position as a reentry planner, which was an increase in pay; however, it was salary, no overtime, and my hours were still during late afternoon. Now I was in a place where I have to fast and pray for guidance and direction. So, I went to my director and informed him of what I wanted to do and the days and hours o f what was needed. It took him a while to come back to me; however, God showed up again, and my hours got changed to what I needed for school. Now, next was my application and money for school. As I informed you earlier, I had been working overtime, so it was not a problem; however, that ceased when I took the new position. Now this was my third time applying for

Living Word School of Ministry, and I had almost given up, as part of the application requested a recommendation for your spouse At this point, my husband and I had been separated approximately five years, and I did not even know where he was or what he was doing. So I put that on the application, and I was honest about the whole situation.

I had trusted in God for this process because I thought they would not let me in because of my separation. I got the call from Minister Aquilla, and she asked me questions about the fivefold ministry; I was so nervous I messed that up, and then she informed me that Pastor Derrick Bright would be calling me to talk with me about the marriage portion of my application. She then requested I come in and take the test, and at that time, Pastor Bright was in the office along with Minster Plummer. Pastor Bright said to me, "Don't look so scared, you are going to be all right." That kind of eased me a little. So then came the interview process with Minister Wendy and Minster Plummer, and it was awesome. I remember her asking me, "Have you ever thought about a ministry name?" I informed her that God had shown me the ministry name GMI (Grace and Mercy International). I told them about the vision God had given me and where the ministry would be. Minister Wendy said, "That is a ministry name." Yes, the question about my separation came up, and I answered it. Minister Plummer said, "Have you thought about getting a divorce?" I replied "no" at that time because I believed in God's will for my marriage. So Minister Wendy said, "Let us pray for your ministry and for God's will for your marriage."

## (KJV) Psalm 118: 8–9
It is better to trust in the Lord than to put confidence in man. It is better to trust in the Lord than to put confidence in princes.

## (KJV) Psalm 40:4
Blessed is the man who makes the Lord his trust, and respecteth

not the proud, to those who turn aside to lies.

**(KJV) Isaiah 30:15**
For thus saith the Lord God, the Holy one of Israel; in returning and rest shall ye be saved; in quietness and in confidence shall be your strength: and ye would not.

**(KJV) Isaiah 26:3**
Thou will keep him in perfect peace, whose mind is stayed on thee; because he trusteth in thee, trust in the Lord forever, for in the Lord JEHOVAH is everlasting strength.

**(KJV) Heremiah 17:7–8**
Blessed is the man that trusteth in the Lord, and whose hope the Lord is; for he shall be like a tree planted by the waters and that spreadteth out her roots by the river, and shall not see when heat cometh, but her leaves shall be green; and shall not be careful in t he year of drought, neither shall cease from yielding fruit.

**Prayer:**
Father God, as we look to You, help us to build our trust in You as we trust man. Help us to trust You in all areas of our lives. Because we know that if we trust You, we can take refuge in You. You are sovereign, God, and we will be even more blessed when we trust You to work it out on our behalf than to allow the enemy to use us falsely and cause us to think that it was from You. Give us strength to stand; in You we are victorious.

# Victorious

Yes, yes, yes, yes, yes! Hallelujah, God, You are awesome, mighty, and wonderful. Lord God, You are my king and my joy and my life, my provider. In You I am victorious. I have the victory in all things. I walk in victory! I live in victory! In You I am victorious, in all things, in every area of my life.

Sorry, I had to take a praise break. Whoo!!!!!

When you know that you know that you know who you are and whose you are, there is nothing you cannot overcome and accomplish. Victory is yours, and all you have to do is believe. You can be victorious in seeking the lost, in your finances, on your job, in your school, in your community, in your home. You are a winner, and God is able to do exceedingly and abundantly above all you can ask or think.

Even now, with me not knowing if we are going to close or not in June, I am still victorious. With all that has happened in the last three months, I am still victorious.

This recession won't break me, and it should not break you. If you continue to read this book and the scriptures I gave you, and fast and pray and believe, then victory shall be yours.

It has not been easy for me these days; however, it has not been hard for me because I relied totally on God for everything. I had to compromise in so many ways; however, He would not let me, and I thank God for that. I did not have to hook or crook, sleep with anyone to make it. I am victorious through Christ.

I thank you for purchasing my book. I know that it will be a blessing for you, as the writing of it has been for me. My life experiences are yours, and I pray that God will increase your faith and wisdom to stand strong and walk in victory. I love you and there is nothing you can do about it.

**Prayer:**
Father, I thank You from the depth of my soul. I have done it and completed what You have given me in this time. I praise You and love You so much. Daddy, I must keep it real; may this book be a blessing to the world, and may it also be a financial blessing to increase my giving. I thank You, God, for walking with me through this whole time. Thank You for breaking the writer's block, thank You for binding the naysayers. I thank You for bringing me back to focus. That even through a marriage breakup, You kept me writing; even through a financial decrease, You kept me writing. Even through the hard times, You kept me writing. God, You even found me a publisher, and I thank You for Tae and I pray that her publishing company will be the top company in the world. I bind every attack that the enemy will bring against her company and me and GMI ministry. I speak prosperity and victory in Jesus' name. I love You so much and I thank You and praise Your name. Hallelujah!!!!!!!!!!!